Lady Bauer in the Tower

Mary Elizabeth Salzmann

Consulting Editor, Diane Craig, M.A./Reading Specialist

ABDO
Publishing Company

Published by ABDO Publishing Company, 4940 Viking Drive, Edina, Minnesota 55435.

Printed in the United States.

Credits
Edited by: Pam Price
Curriculum Coordinator: Nancy Tuminelly
Cover and Interior Design and Production: Mighty Media
Photo and Illustration Credits: BananaStock Ltd., Brand X Pictures, Hemera, Tracy Kompelien, PhotoDisc, Stockbyte

Library of Congress Cataloging-in-Publication Data

Salzmann, Mary Elizabeth, 1968-
    Lady Bauer in the tower / Mary Elizabeth Salzmann.
       p. cm. -- (Rhyme time)
    Includes index.
    ISBN 1-59197-801-7 (hardcover)
    ISBN 1-59197-907-2 (paperback)
    1. English language--Rhyme--Juvenile literature. I. Title. II. Rhyme time (ABDO Publishing Company)

    PE1517.S355 2004
    428.1'3--dc22
                                                                                    2004047366

SandCastle™ books are created by a professional team of educators, reading specialists, and content developers around five essential components that include phonemic awareness, phonics, vocabulary, text comprehension, and fluency. All books are written, reviewed, and leveled for guided reading, early intervention reading, and Accelerated Reader® programs and designed for use in shared, guided, and independent reading and writing activities to support a balanced approach to literacy instruction.

Let Us Know

After reading the book, SandCastle would like you to tell us your stories about reading. What is your favorite page? Was there something hard that you needed help with? Share the ups and downs of learning to read. We want to hear from you! To get posted on the ABDO Publishing Company Web site, send us e-mail at:

sandcastle@abdopub.com

SandCastle Level: Fluent

Words that rhyme do
not have to be spelled the
same. These words rhyme
with each other:

devour

power

flour

scour

flower

shower

glower

sour

hour

tower

Alison is hungry.

She is glad that she has a big sandwich to **devour**.

Diego, Jaden, and their mother picked a beautiful **flower**.

Tammy and Harris are making cookies.

They are covered with **flour**.

You can tell by his **glower** that Shane is upset.

When Corinne and her mom spend time together, they enjoy every **hour**.

Keenan wants to score a goal.

He kicks the ball with all of his **power**.

Food has dried on the plate.

To get it clean, Mary really has to **scour** it.

Loren and her brothers are having fun at a water park.

They play under a **shower**.

Pete, Bridget, and Eden are selling lemonade.

Lemonade is sweet and sour.

Zoey, Sara, and Ronald are
working together to make
a **tower**.

Lady Bauer
in the Tower

There once was a princess named Lady Bauer who was locked up high in a tower.

One day Prince Gower
came to save Lady Bauer.

Said Prince Gower
to Lady Bauer,
"I'll get you out in an hour."

But Prince Gower
did not have the power
to unlock the tower.

To make Lady Bauer
feel less sour,
Prince Gower
gave her a flower.

16

Lady Bauer threw the flower at Prince Gower.

She said, "Instead of a flower, I need something to devour."

So back home went Prince Gower
to bake some bread with wheat flour.

He brought it to the tower
for Lady Bauer.

Then Prince Gower
began to scour
around the tower
to find a way
to save Lady Bauer.

Suddenly, a magic rain shower dropped a key that had special power.

Prince Gower
used the key's power
to unlock the tower
and finally save Lady Bauer.

Rhyming Riddle

What do you call it when it rains lemon juice?

Sour shower

Glossary

devour. to eat quickly and hungrily

glower. a stare expressing anger or annoyance

scour. to scrub something hard in order to clean it; to search thoroughly

tower. a structure or building that is taller than it is wide

water park. an amusement park that has pools, water slides, and other fun activities involving water

About SandCastle™

A professional team of educators, reading specialists, and content developers created the SandCastle™ series to support young readers as they develop reading skills and strategies and increase their general knowledge. The SandCastle™ series has four levels that correspond to early literacy development in young children. The levels are provided to help teachers and parents select the appropriate books for young readers.

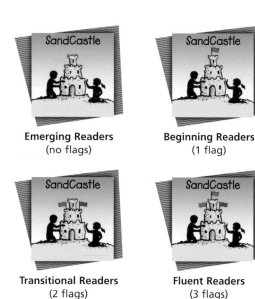

Emerging Readers
(no flags)

Beginning Readers
(1 flag)

Transitional Readers
(2 flags)

Fluent Readers
(3 flags)

These levels are meant only as a guide. All levels are subject to change.

ABDO Publishing Company

To see a complete list of SandCastle™ books and other nonfiction titles from ABDO Publishing Company, visit www.abdopub.com or contact us at:

4940 Viking Drive, Edina, Minnesota 55435 • 1-800-800-1312 • fax: 1-952-831-1632